The Nature Kid's Guide to
RABBITS

RENATA MARIE

LP Media Inc. Publishing

For information address LP Media Inc. Publishing,
3178 253rd Ave. NW, Isanti, MN 55040
www.lpmedia.org

Publication Data

Rabbits
The Nature Kid's Guide to Rabbits — First edition.

Summary: "Learn all about Rabbits, the Nature Kid Way"
— Provided by publisher.

ISBN: 978-1-954288-70-6

[1. Rabbits – Non-Fiction] I. Title.

Title: The Nature Kid's Guide to Rabbits

CONTENTS

FUZZY BUNNIES

Two rabbits climb out of their hole. They hop onto a log to look around.

Rabbits live anywhere they can dig tunnels. They live in forests and meadows. They live in grasslands and wetlands. They live in deserts and cities.

These fuzzy bunnies even make their homes in people's backyards.

DID YOU KNOW?
There are about 30 types of rabbits in the world. They live everywhere, except for Antarctica.

HUGE
HOPPERS

A rabbit thuds through the grass. He is as big as a dog.

Flemish Giant rabbits are the largest rabbits in the world. They can weigh up to 20 pounds (9.1 kilograms) and are 2.5 feet (0.8 meters) long.

Pygmy rabbits are the smallest rabbits in the world. They only weigh one pound (0.5 kg) and are only 12 inches (30 centimeters) long. They are so small that they can fit in a human hand.

Pygmy rabbit

FUN FACT!

One Flemish Giant rabbit weighed 50 pounds (23 kg). That's as much as the average first grader!

EAT AND RUN

A Desert cottontail rabbit hops through a garden. He's looking for a quick snack.

Rabbits are built to eat, spot danger, and escape. Their sharp teeth tear food. Their sharp nails dig holes. Their long ears pick up sounds. Their eyes see almost all around them. Their little noses twitch to help them smell more.

If a **predator** is near, their strong legs hop to safety.

Hare

Rabbit

Rabbits and hares are not the same animals. Hares have longer ears and legs. Their bodies are bigger, and they are faster.

TWITCH AND SNIFF

Twitch! A little nose sniffs for food.

Rabbits use their noses to find food. **They move their noses up and down.** They take in more air and more smells.

Rabbits can smell food that is far away. They can even smell food underground.

DID YOU KNOW?

Rabbit noses are cute. But do not touch them. They can be easily hurt.

TASTY GREENS

Crunch. An Eastern Cottontail snacks on a leaf.

Rabbits are **herbivores**. **They eat plants.** In the summer, they eat grass, clover, and vegetables. They eat weeds, leaves, and flowers.

In the winter, they eat twigs and bark. They eat buds and any plants they can find.

But they are not the only animals looking for food.

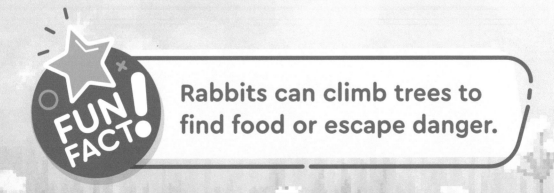

FUN FACT!

Rabbits can climb trees to find food or escape danger.

EARS
UP

Ears stand up. They twist. They turn. They listen for danger.

While rabbits eat, they listen for predators. Their ears stand up. They can turn 270 degrees.

Rabbits also watch for predators. They can see almost 360 degrees around them. They can see above them. They can see behind them.

DID YOU KNOW?

Rabbits cannot see right in front of their noses. They use their noses and ears to learn what is in front of them.

TEETH AND TALONS

Badger

Fox

Owl

Weasel

Wolverine

Thump! A rabbit spots a hawk. He sprints away.

A lot of animals hunt rabbits. Hawks, owls, and eagles hunt them. So do bears, foxes, and wolves. Even weasels, badgers, and wolverines hunt rabbits.

Rabbits have to always be looking out for danger. Their only defense is running away.

DID YOU KNOW?

Rabbits warn other rabbits when they spot danger. They thump their feet on the ground.

HIDDEN HOPPERS

A snowshoe hare stops eating. A wolverine is near.

With so many predators, rabbits need to hide. **Rabbits use camouflage.** Their fur is usually gray and brown. It looks like the land around them.

If a rabbit sees a predator, it holds still and hopes the predator does not spot it. But if it does, the rabbit has one last trick to escape.

FUN FACT!

Pet rabbits can look like wild rabbits. They can also be white, black, striped, or spotted.

ZIGZAG

A fox is near. A rabbit races to his hole.

Rabbits hop with their strong legs. Their fluffy tails are white. They are easy to see. **Predators race after rabbits' tails.** But rabbits know a trick.

Rabbits zigzag. They hop side to side. When they turn, predators lose sight of their tails. They cannot spot the rabbits. And the rabbits slip safely into their holes.

FUN FACT!

Jackrabbits can run up to 45 miles (72 kilometers) per hour.

DIGGING TUNNELS

Whiskers brush dirt. A rabbit digs a hole.

Rabbits use their sharp claws to dig holes. They shovel dirt behind them. They push it out of their holes.

Rabbits have whiskers. **Their whiskers help them feel where they are in the dark.**

Rabbit tunnels have more than one entrance. Tunnels connect with other tunnels, this is called a **warren**. Warrens can be 10 feet (3.0 m) deep.

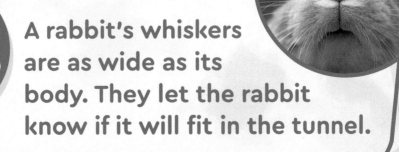

FUN FACT!

A rabbit's whiskers are as wide as its body. They let the rabbit know if it will fit in the tunnel.

BABY BUNNIES

A baby rabbit sleeps in a nest of grass and fur.

Baby rabbits are called kittens. Rabbits can have up to 12 kittens at once. And they can have kittens about five times a year. That is a lot of baby bunnies!

DID YOU KNOW?

Some rabbits make nests in tunnels. Others make nests in small holes. They make them in backyards and gardens.

STAYING SAFE

A mother rabbit leaves the nest. She will not return until the sun sets.

Rabbit kittens are born helpless. They cannot see. They have no fur. Mothers feed their kittens milk.

Mother rabbits only feed their kittens when the sun rises and sets. They do not want predators to follow them to their kittens.

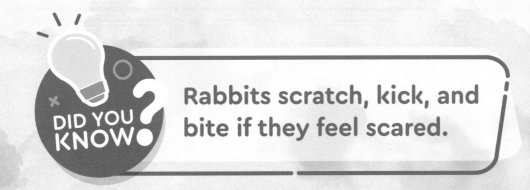

DID YOU KNOW?

Rabbits scratch, kick, and bite if they feel scared.

LEAVING THE NEST

A young rabbit twitches her nose. She leaves her home for the first time.

In three weeks, young rabbits are ready to hop into the world. They dig their own tunnels. They find other rabbits.

Some rabbits live alone. But others live in groups. **A group of rabbits is called a fluffle.** There can be 20 rabbits in a fluffle.

FUN FACT!

Rabbits purr when they are happy. It sounds like teeth chattering.

BOXING BUNNIES

Two rabbits chase each other. They kick, jump, and fight.

Male rabbits chase males. Female rabbits fight females. **They want to show who is in charge.**

Males and females also fight. But they fight to choose a rabbit to make more kittens with.

The female hits the male with her front paws. They bite and chase each other. They even jump over each other.

DID YOU KNOW?

Rabbits run in circles, honk, and grunt when they want to make more kittens.

CUTE
AND QUIET

A rabbit hops up to a kid. She wants to be petted.

Not all rabbits are wild. **People keep rabbits as pets.** They are cute and quiet. They come in many colors and sizes.

Pet rabbits may act like wild rabbits. But pet rabbits should never live in the wild. They are not as scared. They will not run away as quickly. And predators are not the only dangers out there.

DID YOU KNOW?

A long time ago, people began keeping rabbits as farm animals. They wanted them for their meat and fur.

PLANT PESTS

A Netherland Dwarf rabbit sneaks into a garden. She munches on flowers.

Rabbits live all over the world. Sometimes they help the land and animals. Rabbits are food for many animals. They also eat plants that could take over. They spread plant seeds.

But in other places, rabbits are pests. They eat plants that other animals eat. They take over spaces that other animals call home.

DID YOU KNOW?

Sometimes rabbits eat people's plants in gardens. To keep them out, put a fence around the garden. Or sprinkle hot peppers around the plants. They are too spicy for rabbits.

TO HELP OR NOT TO HELP

A tiny rabbit hops through the grass, but she is not lost.

Sometimes people want to help wild rabbits. But wild rabbits usually do not need help.

People find kittens in nests. But they are usually not alone. Mother rabbits may be nearby.

People find young rabbits. They may be small, but they no longer need care.

If a person finds a hurt rabbit, they can take it to a wildlife care center.

DID YOU KNOW?

If a human spots a pet rabbit in the wild, they should call a nearby animal **shelter**.

HOPPILY EVER AFTER

A rabbit hops after his fluffle.

Some types of rabbits are in danger of dying out. Humans are building on their land. Fires are burning their homes.

But people are trying to help. They create new homes for rabbits. They try to keep them safe. They want these cute creatures to live happily ever after.

DID YOU KNOW?

Do not move a lost rabbit to a new place. It could be hit by a car or spotted by a predator.

GLOSSARY

camouflage
something that helps
an animal hide
page 18

herbivores
animals that
eat plants
page 13

fluffle
a group of rabbits
that live
together
page 29

predator
animals that hunt
other animals
page 8

shelter
a safe place
page 37

warren
connected tunnels
where rabbits live
page 23

MORE AMAZING ANIMAL BOOKS
from Nature Kids Publishing!

The Nature Kid's Guide to
PANDAS
Level 2

A LEVEL 2 READER FOR CURIOUS YOUNG **KIDS** WHO LOVE PANDA BEARS!

RENATA MARIE

The Nature Kid's Guide to
MEERKATS
Level 2

A LEVEL 2 READER FOR CURIOUS YOUNG **KIDS** WHO LOVE MEERKATS!

RENATA MARIE

The Nature Kid's Guide to
CHEETAHS
Level 2

A LEVEL 2 READER FOR CURIOUS YOUNG **KIDS** WHO LOVE CHEETAHS!

RENATA MARIE

The Nature Kid's Guide to
GIRAFFES
Level 2

A LEVEL 2 READER FOR CURIOUS YOUNG **KIDS** WHO LOVE GIRAFFES!

RENATA MARIE

Visit NatureKidsPublishing.com to Learn More!

Made in United States
Troutdale, OR
02/01/2024

17340617R10026